# The Worthy Way

# THE WORTHY WAY

## Memoirs of a Pioneer Black Law Enforcement Officer

By Arthur G. Worthy

NewSouth Books
Montgomery | Louisville

NewSouth Books
105 South Court Street
Montgomery, AL 36104

This book was
edited by Jacqueline Allen Trimble
and proofread by Dr. Leon Donaldson
and Michael Worthy.

ISBN-13: 978-1-60306-034-9
ISBN-10: 1-60306-034-0

Printed in the United States of America

The author's proceeds from this book
are being donated by the Worthy Family to
the William Kid Franklin Boys and Girls Club,
Community Congregational United Church of
Christ, First Baptist Church, and Highland
Avenue Baptist Church.

TO MY LOVELY WIFE

## MILDRED

WHO HAS BEEN MY LOVE, AND MY FRIEND

FOR FORTY-NINE YEARS.

SHE IS GOD'S GREATEST BLESSING TO ME.

# Contents

WHEREAS:    We the employees of the U. S. Marshals Service, Middle
            District of Alabama.

WHEREAS:    Some of us having known Arthur Worthy for some fourteen
            years.

WHEREAS:    Watching him work for those years.

WHEREAS:    Knowing he is retiring this date.

WHEREAS:    Knowing his wonderful wife Mildred and for her kindness
            and consideration.

WHEREAS:    Knowing she will now have to put up with him all the time.

WHEREAS:    Knowing she will not put up with the kind of work and goof-
            offs as the Marshals Service has.

THEREFORE:  The employees of the U. S. Marshals Service of the Middle
            District of Alabama presents this local Funeral Home Gift
            Certificate good for 90 days to the wonderful wife of said
            Arthur George Worthy.

BECAUSE:    If he works for her as he has for the Marshals Service,
            she will need it.

WHEREAS:    We of the Middle District having kidded, pulled tricks and
            aggravated the said Arthur George Worthy more than anyone
            in the office.

THEREFORE:  We lay aside the WHEREAS and THEREFORES and say to one of
            the greatest and best friends we have and probably will
            ever know --- The best of luck, a long and happy life,
            and this office will never be the same after this day.
            We love you Arthur George Worthy.

# FOREWORD

O ME, LIFE IS not as complicated as we make it. Spiritual, social, financial, and even moral successes are ours for the having. I write these memoirs to show young people that there are approaches that can be applied to life's most difficult situations and those approaches will lead to success. My life has taught me the truth of this statement. I have had experiences in three of the most difficult areas of human relations: law enforcement, education, and racial conflict. I also know something of economic survival. Over the past seventy-one years, I have done things the Arthur Worthy way, and that way has not created a single enemy. My secret? I have learned to live with other people. These memoirs emphasize some of the experiences that shaped my life and acknowledge that the Supreme Being bestowed upon me whatever understanding of human relations I have.

9

# THE WORTHY WAY

# INTRODUCTION

THIS MEMOIR is not about my early life. That's another story. But I suppose it is always good to say something about one's beginning.

I was born in rural Marengo County, Alabama, in 1929. My parents were Joe and Nancy Worthy. I had seven sisters and five brothers. I grew up on a large farm where it was my responsibility to make the fires in our four fireplaces and to carry water and food to the field for the others so they could keep working as long as possible.

I went to school in a one-room schoolhouse until I was in the seventh grade. I still remember some of the poems I learned at that time. I didn't have to study too much. I learned from the upper classes by listening to them recite.

In the eighth and ninth grades, I went to boarding school. That was how it was for us then. There was no public transportation for black children in Alabama. From tenth grade on, though, the county paid a black man who owned a bus to transport us children to school. After graduating from Linden Academy, I enrolled in Selma University for my junior college training. I lived with a family and paid them five dollars a week for a room and one meal a day. Since I couldn't afford to pay for anything but dinner, I used to leave home early so I wouldn't have to smell the breakfast cooking.

When I graduated from the junior college, I joined the United States Army. It was after my discharge from the service that I married Mildred James.

# I

# HOW IT ALL BEGAN

DECIDING JUST WHERE to start this writing was more difficult than making myself get started. I thought of beginning with incidents before high school or my first real job after the army or ten other events that marked some important start in my life. I knew, though, that I had to begin with my wife of forty-eight years, Mildred. Beginning my memoirs without beginning with her would be unrealistic.

Mildred and I met while I was in the army, and we wrote each other every day for the ten months I was in Germany. On October 28, 1952, I received my Certificate of Service. The Korean Conflict was still going on, and my discharge was not issued until some two years later. Soon after returning home to Linden, Alabama, I began to get ready for the big day, Mildred's and my wedding. By November 10th we were in Bennettsville, South Carolina, getting married. It would take a whole chapter to explain why Bennettsville, South Carolina, but let's just say that anywhere else we would have had to wait two weeks after applying for a license to get married. We couldn't wait. We wed in the County Courthouse. Mildred's uncle and the Probate Judge's secretary were the only witnesses. The next night there was a party at Grandmother's house with most of the church members attending. Even the mother of the old boyfriend everybody thought Mildred would marry attended, but instead of Mildred James Gunn she had become Mildred James Worthy. I think they all realized that there was nothing wrong with her being a Worthy in name since everyone who knew her considered her worthy in character.

From the beginning, our marriage taught me a great deal about human nature. I am a brown-skinned black man and my wife is a very fair black woman. At the time we got married, race and skin color were quite important. I do not really find it less so now. I sometimes wonder who resented our being together more, blacks or whites. Right after I became one of the first black policemen in Montgomery, Alabama, Mildred and I went to town to buy furniture one afternoon after I had dressed for work. As we walked down Monroe Street, everyone that we met, black and white, turned and stared at us. They all seemed to be wondering: *Is this a white man that has turned black? This can't be a black man because there are no black policemen, and no black man would dare walk down Monroe Street with a blonde hanging on his arm.* I became so self-conscious that I began feeling the stares.

I told Mildred, "If I get you home, I'll never come downtown with you again while in this police uniform."

White males seemed to think we were just unreal. Another time, some years later, when we were being stared at by a white man, I said to him in a teasing manner, "This ain't what you think, Mister. This is not a blonde; this is a North

Carolina redbone." When he saw my U.S. Marshal's service revolver on my side, he accepted it as a big joke. He laughed and implied he was not really staring at us. These days, black women seem to resent seeing Mildred and me together as much as white men once did. I think that is because of a feeling in the black community, particularly among women of the lower socioeconomic class, that a black man who dates or marries a white woman is a racial traitor. If that man is financially secure, that feeling is multiplied. This is partly because there is reported to be a shortage of marriageable black men for the available population of black women, and that is partly because of the abnormally high rates of incarceration and premature death among black males.

When Mildred and I first got married I was a student at Alabama State College (now Alabama State University). In fact, it was there I got the idea to go into law enforcement. One day in Negro History class, Dr. Norman Walton said, "You know the City of Montgomery is trying to hire some Negro policemen, but everyone is afraid to apply for the job."

I jumped up in class and said, "I'm not afraid of anything or anybody."

Dr. Walton said, "If that is true, go down to Professor Pierce's room and give him your name." I stood up and started out of the room, really with the intention of leaving class early and making a legal cut. But Dr. Walton preceded me to Professor Pierce's room, calling my bluff.

When we entered the room, he introduced me as a candidate for the Negro policeman's job to Professor Pierce, who then said, "Fine. Here, take these papers and fill them out and return them to City Hall where it is indicated thereon." I took the papers and was immediately curious. The more I read, the more I liked the idea of becoming a policeman.

That afternoon I discussed the papers with Mildred. I was very surprised to find that she, too, seemed interested in my completing and submitting the job application. I later said that Mildred's interest was because she had grown sick of living on our small student's budget. Things were so tight with us that we knew exactly where every penny of my $130 GI check was going, down to twelve cents for the parking meter. We couldn't even afford to spend the forty-six cents it would have cost for a night at the movie theater. For recreation we would go for drives in the country on Sunday afternoons. Gasoline was only twenty-nine cents a gallon at the time. The car note was $51.02 and the rent was $30. Tuition was $42 per quarter, which came to $14 per month. Allowing five dollars for books, we had $46.96 left to spend each month. When I said we had a tight budget, I was not exaggerating. Before our daughter Carol was born, we had to save money for a three-day hospital stay and for the doctor's bill. There was no such thing as health insurance in our budget.

We also had to get Mildred's tuition out of this budget since she, too, was enrolled in college before the baby came. Prior to our marriage we had discussed her going back to school and getting her college degree. I told her that she had too much natural talent to just sit by and be a housewife. Mildred finished as valedictorian of the Lillington, North Carolina, Shawtown High School graduating class of 1951. One of the reasons that I was so interested in Mildred's getting a college degree was so that she could get a teaching job, one of the few respectable professions available to blacks at that time.

I never pictured myself getting middle-aged. I thought that I would die while still in my thirties, leaving Mildred with two or three children to raise. I'm not sure why I felt this way, but I did.

This was before the time of McDonald's, Hardee's and other fast-food businesses. If Mildred had no formal training or a teacher's certificate, she would have to take a maid's job to support the children. Blondes were not in high demand for the position of housemaid. So, we decided Mildred would enroll in college. We hoped that she would make all A's because if she did she could get a President's Scholarship and her tuition would be free. The one major obstacle to our plan was a course called Science that was taught by Dr. Benjamin Hatcher. Almost everybody failed it and had to take it a second time. Mildred made all A's the first quarter, and all the other faculty members were anxious to meet the student that made an A in Dr. Hatcher's Science class.

Before Carol was born, we roomed with a couple, but I vowed I would not have a child born while living in someone else's house. We moved out and the rent went from $30 to $35. Plus, we now had utilities to pay. I took a job as a dishwasher at the Standard Country Club, an establishment of rich Jewish people. It was here I came to realize that during that era blacks were just one of the many racial groups that were looked down upon in America. That's another story.

Back to our tight budget. No one was more acutely aware of our financial circumstances than Mildred. It is little wonder she was so receptive to the idea of my being employed as a policeman. I completed my application and submitted it to the proper authorities. Within a short time, I was contacted and told to report for the written examination. I expected that there would be some questions about law enforcement, at least a few. I took the exam and was somewhat surprised that it was so simple. The questions were of a general nature like those of a standard intelligence test. I never knew my score, but over the years one of the leaders of the black community who had been behind the whole idea implied several times that my score had been almost perfect. Not having a military police background, and being an unknown from the "country," I knew that something had impressed the group. I did not realize, however, until some time after I had been hired and was working, just how important being a "Montgomery" boy was in the black community.

I answered a police call one night, and after completing the business (I don't remember what it was) the lady of the house engaged me in conversation.

"Where are you from, young man?" she asked, after a bit of talk.

"I'm from Marengo County," I said.

"Marengo County?" she said. "I think it's just awful they didn't give your job to a *Montgomery* boy."

What can only be described as a rookie school was set up for the eight of us who made the highest scores on the examination. I'm not sure what they called it really. Being black, we did not go to school where all the regular policemen went. Mixing of the races was a violation of the law at the time. What a farce the whole issue of segregation was! —sometimes more political than actual feeling. Our rookie school was taught at the old "colored" library on Union Street. I believe it was later considered a community center. Some of our instructors also taught the white recruits at the regular police school; we had some of the heavyweights because this was a new venture and everybody wanted things to be just right. "We've got to get these niggers off on the right foot," I imagine they said to themselves. There were interesting aspects to being a sworn officer of the law. No wonder whites had kept this area of work exclusively for themselves.

During the instruction, no one actually said it, but it was made quite plain that nobody could instruct a sworn law enforcement officer to ignore a crime committed in his presence. To ignore a crime would be a violation of his oath of office. Therefore, no superior could instruct me to violate my oath. This charge to uphold the law was emphasized to the black policemen more than once.

Therefore, while we pioneering black police officers were assigned to patrol black neighborhoods so we would have as little opportunity as possible to come in contact with white lawbreakers, we had the authority to arrest whites.

Sometimes the radio dispatcher would publish an APB (all points bulletin) then instruct us to telephone him. He would then stress that we were also expected to be on the lookout for the wanted suspect. On one or two occasions after an APB was put out, the supervisor called our unit to ask for a meeting with us. During this meeting he would instruct us the same way the radio dispatcher had. Neither the supervisor nor the dispatcher would say it explicitly, but there was no question both meant, "This means you, too."

One of the things our training instructor used to say was, "Fellows, be very careful when it comes to women because everybody wants to go to bed with a policeman." The longer I was a policeman, the more I found this to be true. Race was no exception. Some things I found out about sexual race mixing from a legal position during the days of intense

segregation would blow a person's mind, but I dare not
mention them here in my memoirs because they were not part
of my experiences, and there is no way of proving what I
learned. Realizing that many facts relating to human relations
and segregation were not as they had been portrayed to the
general public shocked me. The further I moved forward in
my life the more I understood that feelings and attitudes could
be very deceptive. The fact that man is an emotional being
causes words to come across the way they do. For example, the
minister appeals to his listeners' emotions rather than to their
reason and common sense because this is the easiest way to get
their attention. Likewise, the politician does the very same
thing with the race card in playing the political game. Politics
is not played any differently now that there are a number of
blacks holding office. Our children are the subjects of the
same old racial emotional appeal as always, and you can bet
your life it works on adults as well as our little children.

There I go straying from the story a bit. I know that
memoirs are supposed to be ordered and orderly. I know that
I start with one story and tell another. Maybe I ramble a bit.
But this is the Arthur Worthy way of writing memoirs, and
the whole point of this is to share who I am and what my
experiences have taught me. Look, you are dealing with a
personality that has always done things just a little differently.
When I was a U.S. Deputy Marshal, I had a grand jury
indictment warrant for a well-known banker on a charge of
bank fraud, which was a federal offense. I phoned him and
said, "I would rather not come to your business and do this in
the presence of your employees as this could be very embar-
rassing. After all, you have not been proven guilty . . . yet.
Come down to my office on the second floor of the Post

Office and Federal Court House at Court and Lee streets." I made a practice of calling people and letting them know I had an arrest warrant for them and telling them to come to my office to avoid having to embarrass them on their jobs. I did this with success more than just once or twice. A similar incident occurred when a county sheriff was charged with violating a recently passed federal statute concerning election fraud. I told him that I was not about to arrest a fellow law enforcement officer without respecting him enough to allow him to surrender. Both of these men were most grateful to me for the manner in which I handled their arrests.

The sheriff said, "I'm damn glad those damn FBI's didn't get the warrant. They would have been happy to put hand-cuffs on me and take me away."

I even arrested a street drunk one night when I was still a policeman and upon approaching the jail, he looked at me and said, "Mr. Police, I'm glad you're putting me in jail."

I said to him, "You're drunker than I thought you were. Why are you glad I'm putting you in jail?"

He said, "You know, you're the first policeman that has ever called me 'Mister.'"

A week or two earlier, I had picked him up at Decatur Street Grill. He was a regular customer. In other words, each Monday morning he was in the Recorder's Court paying a fine for public drunkenness in the streets. I felt sorry for him. "If I take you home, will you stay there until you're sober?" I asked.

"Yes, sir" he said. "I'll get in bed and go to sleep." I took him home to an address in Paterson Court, just two blocks away. I thought to myself, *that was a good deed*, and went about my patrol duties.

About an hour later, I got a call from the radio operator: "Car #16, Decatur Street Grill, signal 99/72." The "signal 99" was investigation and the "signal 72" meant that an ambulance would be coming. Someone probably had been cut or shot. Upon arriving at the Decatur Street Grill, I found the man I thought I had done the good deed for an hour or so earlier lying on the ground, bleeding from several stab wounds.

The first thing he said was, "He took all my money. I haven't bought any groceries or paid my rent." The ambulance had not arrived. Because he was suffering, I called the radio operator and advised him that we would be taking the victim to St. Jude Hospital. When I saw it was the man I had taken home instead of arresting, I thought *I will not make the mistake again of thinking I am doing a drunk a good deed.*

The Montgomery Police Department was an eye-opener for me on life in general. I did not realize that there was so much I did not know. I also learned that there was quite a bit the general public does not know. When we went to the street the first time as police officers, Sergeant Mills, Sergeant Stephens, or Sergeant Williams, men who were all very good in individual ways, accompanied us, as our training officer. Sergeant Mills was, perhaps, the most admired because of his teaching methods. His favorite words were, "You ain't seen nothing yet!" He would always say this when we had experienced something new like a shooting and killing or an extreme domestic disturbance between a husband and wife. Although Sergeant Mills was not a college graduate or an educated man, he was a self-taught psychologist, which is so very important when it comes to understanding people.

During this period of on-the-job teaching from the various sergeants, we really saw something when certain out-of-town entertainers such as Little Willie Johns, B. B. King, Percy Mayfield, and others played at Club 400. The club was for "Colored" (as black people were called then), but there would always be several white couples present. (As I have already said this race-mixing was illegal.) Club 400 was owned and operated by a white man who apparently had some influence with the city government. Dances at the club were always worked by off-duty white police officers, so somebody at city hall had to know what was going on, even though *everybody* did not know what was going on. There was a white lieutenant who certainly did not know, and his ignorance almost got him into trouble. This lieutenant usually worked administration, but on this particular occasion, for some reason, he got assigned to the second shift supervising patrol division. One night, he checked on Club 400 and found it to be operated on a Sunday night by a white man that he said did not have an operating license. He immediately called my partner and me. When we arrived at the scene, he ordered us to seize custody of the operator and take him to headquarters. When we arrived at the station, the operator of the club called one of the off-duty captains. He came immediately. The lieutenant explained to the captain why he had charged the operator.

The captain said, "I'm not sure just what kind of license he's got, but you turn him loose, and just watch him."

I said to my partner, "Watch. That lieutenant will be back in administration tomorrow." Sure enough, the next day or so the lieutenant was out of the patrol division and back behind a desk.

The sergeants who were our training officers would always go into the restaurants and sit at the tables and eat with us when mealtime came or it was time for a sandwich. On the west side of town, we ate at the Raven Drive Inn Restaurant. On the east side, we would eat at Wimpy's Play House Restaurant. All food at both places was on-the-house for the police. We were told that accepting food was not in violation of the law or any police regulations and that Gaston Bell, who owned and operated Wimpy's Play House, and Nurse Addie Payne, who owned The Raven, were good friends of the police department. Nurse Payne also owned and operated Oak Street General Hospital. I never really knew the deal between Addie Payne, Gaston Bell, and the Montgomery Police Department, other than feeding all police officers who worked their districts, but I always felt that there was something else going on. Policemen always sent blacks who were shot or stabbed to Oak Street General Hospital. In later years, something also came to light where certain police officers would issue a traffic ticket and tell the violator to go to Gaston Bell because he would take care of the matter. Eventually it came to light that Gaston Bell and some office workers downtown had been involved in ticket fixing.

I mentioned earlier the farce of segregation. Here's an experience that illustrates my point. One day when we went to work, our training sergeants told us that they could no longer go into restaurants with us when we stopped to eat.

"Has anybody complained about your presence in colored restaurants?" I asked.

"No," one sergeant said, "but our supervisors said since we can't take you into the Elite Restaurant because its for whites only then it is not fair for us to go with you into black restaurants."

The supervisors instructed the white policemen to sit in

the police car and eat their meals while we were inside. This practice was in keeping with the state and city segregation laws. To show just how foolish the whole practice was, a "black" foreign officer who was stationed at Maxwell Air Force Base could go into any of the downtown white restaurants and get served. Black maids could accompany the white children she was baby-sitting into any whites-only theater. Segregation laws had more to do with control than feelings or beliefs.

I enjoyed my work to the fullest. Then, after I had been a police officer for about two and a half years, an incident occurred that changed the course of history as well as the course of my life. Rosa Parks refused to give up her seat on the Washington Park city bus to a white man and was arrested for violation of the City of Montgomery laws. This arrest set off an immediate reaction in the black community. Rosa Parks called E. D. Nixon to get her out of jail by signing her bond. However, Nixon went to work planning and organizing a black technique for dealing with the situation.

Although Nixon was not a Rhodes Scholar, perhaps not even a high school graduate, he was a man of great intelligence with a heart as big as all Montgomery. The most unusual thing about E. D. Nixon was his ability to know who would be best to take the limelight or leadership role in such a situation. His vast knowledge led him to Martin Luther King, Jr., the young minister at the Dexter Avenue Baptist Church, who was thought to be a fiery speaker. Even though King was relatively new in the Montgomery Community, he was well respected.

A mass meeting was scheduled for all blacks. It was well-advertised to be held at Holt Street Baptist Church for

Monday, December 5, 1955. The city fathers and the police department became very concerned because of all the publicity that this announcement received. The black police officers were called into headquarters to meet with some very high city officials, including the chief. We were instructed to report to the Holt Street Baptist Church at the designated time and take notes as to what went on. Following the mass meeting we were to report back to headquarters and make a written report—our impression of what had gone on.

I found myself sitting in the back of the church in police uniform making mental notes on everything, including the various speakers. Of all the meetings that I had attended during my lifetime up to that point, I had never seen so many serious expressions on the faces of my people. Everyone that I observed had a look that said *you are in the class with the oppressor: the police.*

After the meeting, we went back to police headquarters as we had been previously instructed to do. We were designated a special room in which to go and do our reports. When I was sure that we were alone, I said to the other three officers, "We've got to make these reports as objective as possible. In your sentences be sure to say 'they' and whatever you do, don't say 'we'. All eyes are going to be on us, the black policemen. The least thing we do is going to be blown out of proportion."

We decided, further, that if it seemed we were in any way involved in the movement, we would be in trouble job-wise. I said, "Let's not show sympathy with the movement to our superiors or our white co-workers or we're in *trouble.*" I felt that if the bus boycott were a success, they would use our dismissal or firing to get back at the black community if it could be determined that we black policemen were in any way being used by the movement.

Of course the Montgomery Bus Boycott turned out to be very successful. I always thought it was because of a tactical error made by the city fathers or the police department. It was highly publicized by the department and the city that a police patrol car would be following the Washington Park and the South Jackson Street buses, both of which had an eighty to ninety percent black patronage, to protect anyone who wanted to ride those buses. This was, in fact, done, but the black leadership anticipated correctly what needed to be done to counteract this action. The black leaders knew that there would be some blacks, particularly very poor blacks, who would ride the buses even though most of the community had agreed to boycott at the mass meeting. They knew the average poor black person thought police presence meant "arrest" not "protection," so the leaders placed someone from the movement at certain strategic locations and bus stops.

On the first day of the proposed boycott, there were a few who intended to ride. However, when the buses came along being followed by patrol cars with two white police officers, the strategically-placed boycotters would yell out, "If you get on that bus those white policemen will put you in jail!" When the would-be bus rider would hear this, he or she would run away. The leadership knew that if anyone rode others would join him or her and lessen the effect of the boycott. It was always my contention that had the police department and the city fathers decided to put black policemen behind the buses, the intended riders would have felt less threatened. This is not necessarily true, I must admit, but again, this is Arthur Worthy's perception.

There was one lady who lived on South Holt Street who

was not frightened by those who had been strategically located at the bus stops, and she rode the bus anyway. Very soon she received threats on her life. She reported the threats to the police department, and I found myself spending numerous shifts in front of her home. Our supervisor told us that it was important that nothing happened to this lady or we would be in serious trouble. I was very uncomfortable with this assignment because the house did not have a driveway from the front. Someone could have come from behind the house, and we would never have seen him. I have often wondered if there were any actual threats or if she made the report because she anticipated threats. She knew that such a report would get an immediate response from the police department.

There seemed to have been a conscientious effort on the part of the department not to put the black police officers in the position of having to arrest our people for breaking the segregation laws. Shortly after it was apparent the boycott would be successful, black leaders were arrested in mass for violation of the century-old Alabama Anti-boycott law. Not one leader was arrested by a black police officer. The effort may have been not to put us in an awkward position. But there again you have Arthur Worthy's approach to life's problems. I try to see good in everything and everybody. I realize that some others can only see evil in any act by Southern whites of that period in history. I respect those who have different viewpoints. Many would question how I, a person who has come in contact with some of the worst elements in our society, am still able to see good in everyone he has had contact with. To keep from getting ahead of myself, as I am about to do, I will say more later about the basis of my feeling that there is some good in everyone.

Back to the boycott. Very soon incidents occurred that confirmed I was right in my feeling that the slightest involvement in the movement would put our jobs on the line.

After the training sergeants had finished riding with us, one of the black recruits, W. C. "Trees" Miller, was drafted into the military and was replaced by Charlie Prather. After the successful boycott, we were taken out of police control cars. Prather and Lee Ernest Jarrett were assigned a walking beat downtown, and Walter Jarrett and I were assigned to ride bicycles on the west side of town.

Other things began happening that let me know that job security should be kept in mind. Prather was fired for allegedly disobeying a direct order. His sergeant had supposedly told him to stand on the corner of Monroe and Lawrence streets and not to leave his position. It was said that Prather walked around the block. He never denied it, but such an order was most unusual, and he was fired for disobeying. After we were reassigned patrol cars on the west side, I received a call to go to the city jail because someone there wanted to see me. I drove the patrol car to the facility just off North Ripley Street. I asked the jail supervisor if he knew who wanted to see me. He didn't know so I waited there a good thirty minutes. No one came.

Finally, I called the radio dispatcher and asked if there were any further word from the person who had called for me. He said, "If he isn't there yet, just go back to your patrol district."

We started for the west side. As we were going up the hill at the end of Montgomery Street, we heard a loud explosion. I said, "They finally got him."

We headed straight for Cleveland Avenue (now Rosa

Parks Avenue). Sure enough, when we arrived at the Lutheran church, a crowd had gathered. A bomb had exploded in front of the residence of Reverend Robert Graetz, a white minister, and his family. The fact that he headed a black congregation was an indication that he was a black sympathizer, and the supporters of segregation targeted him. Recently, Graetz wrote a book, *A White Preacher's Memoir*. In this book he tells about these bombings and his activities in the movement. He was the only white minister in Montgomery who supported the bus boycott.

At the time, being the only one working and with a wife still in college, I had to think very seriously about job security even though I enjoyed my work as a law enforcement officer. *After all*, I said to myself, *Arthur George, you have a college degree in elementary education and you have a wife and two little children to care for.* It was very obvious to us, the black police officers, that the beat-walking downtown and the bicycle patrolling on the west side were nothing more than attempts to get back at the black leadership through retaliation against the black police officers who were the only city workers who did not have a menial, traditional "colored" job. I am convinced that the leadership at the police department had no negative feelings toward black policemen in general. Their actions were aimed at the black leadership.

Even though Walter Jarrett and I were put back in patrol cars, things were never the same. In previous times, we would make at least ten arrests for public drunkenness and five to ten arrests for fighting on a typical weekend. After the boycott, some weekends we did not make a single arrest. I became concerned that officials would think we were ignoring violations by blacks, so I asked an officer with whom I had become friendly, how he was doing in arrests. I was surprised that he and his partner were experiencing the very same thing. The Montgomery Bus Boycott had made a completely different society in the black community. Some of the old weekly drunks told me that they were attending church every Sunday. The movement had a very positive effect. The weekly mass meetings had blacks that had never gone to church before going to church on Sundays. It was unreal to see the general change of attitudes that took place in the black community throughout Montgomery.

I was ready for a change in my own life, too. I contacted the Superintendent of Education for Montgomery County and was sent to Mr. W. S. Garrett for an interview. During the interview I was told that all applicants for a position in the Montgomery County School System must have a "B" average for their college work. I told him I understood and felt I could meet those standards. I was given forms to complete and return to the Board of Education. Soon after my forms were received, I was called in by Mr. Garrett for another interview. This time he told me my total points did not add up to a "B" average. I explained to him that I was a transfer student from Selma University where I had attended junior college. When a student transferred, the receiving college would only give the student a "C" for all grades up to that point. He did not understand, but luckily his secretary did and explained it to him. He then told me to go to Booker T. Washington High School and tell Rawles H. Dobbins that he had sent me. *A change is coming now, Arthur George*, I thought. The talk with R. H. Dobbins turned out to be quite interesting. Dobbins told me that if the "Man" had sent me to talk with him, I was as good as hired. Dobbins had been designated principal of the new Mary Foster McDavid Elementary School. I later learned that Dobbins had been the first sergeant in a military company where Garrett had been the commanding officer during World War II. *I should have been the company clerk,* I thought. *I would have it made.* But I was just a little too young for World War II.

Things started moving exceedingly fast. Before I knew it, it was September and I found myself in an entirely new environment. I had to clean up my language to comply with the demands of my new profession. I said to myself, *Arthur George, this ain't the Day and Greyhound street folk. You can't be saying hell and damn in every sentence. Clean up your act, fellow. Remember that you are in charge of children, who are delicate and easily hurt.* On a number of occasions I found myself struggling to control my language.

I had the students correcting each other's papers and one of the children asked, "Mr. Worthy, if Kenneth spelled history H-I-S-T-O-R-I-E, should I mark it right or wrong?"

Before I could think I replied, "Hell, yes." Then I thought about where I was. I was no longer a policeman. No more arresting drunks, or dealing with shooting and stabbing. I looked at the children. Then, I started trying to erase what I had just said by smoothing it over with an elaboration in more appropriate words.

# II

# THE HIRING OF BLACKS
# AS DEPUTY U.S. MARSHALS

A BOUT 1962 OR LATE 1963, there went out a cry for black U.S. Deputy Marshals. Federal District Court ordered the University of Mississippi to enroll James Meredith, and he had to be protected. About the only Southern state with a black Deputy U.S. Marshal was Tennessee. Tennessee had three Federal Judicial Districts: the eastern district in Knoxville, the middle district in Nashville, and the western district in Memphis. The western district hired E. Frank Lamondue as the first black Deputy U.S. Marshal sometime during 1960. Perhaps the next Southern district was the middle district of North Carolina at Greensboro. This might have been Joseph C. Biggers. I know that he was one of the earlier ones.

Attorney Fred Gray, whom I knew from my policing days since he had handled most of the legal work of the boycott, contacted me. I did not realize that getting employed in this federal position was so political. Perhaps I put too much emphasis on James Meredith's integration of the University of Mississippi as the basis for the demand of black Deputy U.S. Marshals in the South. I have no proof, but one must not underestimate the influence of Judge Frank M. Johnson, Jr. on my being hired in the middle district of Alabama. In all probability, Judge Johnson noticed the absence of black marshals and blacks period in the federal courts. He no doubt said to himself, *I can't order state and local officials to integrate when the United States District Court doing the ordering is lily white.*

A black deputy clerk was hired in the district clerk's office and a black secretary was hired in the probation office. It seems that I remember some contact being made between the Judge and Mrs. A. G. Gaston for secretaries when the secretary was hired for the U.S. Probation Office. I think that person was from the Birmingham area. We were all hired during the same time period. As I said, I have no proof, but I feel that Judge Frank M. Johnson approached Attorney Gray when Deputy U.S. Marshals were being sought for employment in the district. You may ask why a person with my background would not want the actual facts stated. I can only answer, *This is Arthur Worthy's version of what took place. It is not research, but writing from the heart.* Another statement of which I have no absolute proof is that Judge Johnson had FBI agents that he personally assigned investigate my background. At least, this is what I was told by some of my old acquaintances in Marengo County where I grew up. According to them, two sets of FBI agents came through asking questions at two different times about Arthur G. Worthy. Surely Judge Frank Johnson sent one of these groups. It is, in my opinion, the only way that he would have personally recommended me to United States Marshal Service (USMS) headquarters in Washington, D.C.

Attorney Gray had me complete employment application

form #57. This form was submitted to the Alabama Democratic Conference, which was chaired by Attorney Orzell Billingsley, Jr. He informed me in a letter dated May 26, 1964, that my application had been forwarded to the Democratic National Committee. It was unbelievable to me that such was the procedure for obtaining federal employment. Years later I would come to realize just how political the system really was.

After it was certain that I would be hired, Billingsley called me and asked me to meet him in Birmingham to discuss the matter of being a Deputy U.S. Marshal. Instead of meeting in his office, we met on Eighth Avenue in front of a well-known building. In his conversation, he told me that I was not the first black. Deputy Elijah Hill had been hired in Birmingham and was the first in the state of Alabama. Hill came to Montgomery from time to time to bring prisoners to the Federal Prison Camp at Maxwell AFB. He said he would tell Hill to contact me the next time he came to Montgomery to brief me on what to expect. The Southern politicians were very careful in who was selected. Most of the blacks that were hired in the earlier years were college graduates.

Soon after that meeting I received a communication from the Director of the United States Marshal Service telling me to report on Monday, August 3, 1964, to United States Marshal William M. Parker, Jr., for duty at the United States Marshal's Office at the Federal Building on the second floor of the downtown post office building at Lee and Court streets. Meanwhile, one of the local newspapers printed the article "Deputy U.S. Marshal Quits Job Here; Blasts Federal Policy on Race." In this article details were given about my hiring as the first black Deputy U.S. Marshal in Montgomery, Alabama.

I must digress for a moment. When my application was submitted, it had to be accompanied by a set of fingerprints. I was told to go to a local law enforcement agency and request someone make the fingerprints. I became so concerned about what the local agencies would do to counteract my employment, I decided to go to the Military Police at Maxwell Air Force Base.

The newspaper article was published about a week before I was to report for duty. Upon seeing this publication, I took the family on vacation so that I would not be present for a response in case the press tried to contact me. I wanted to avoid the media at all costs. I felt that the less that was published about me, the better. I did not want the Klan and other white supremacy groups to become too interested in my being hired as the first black Deputy Marshal in Montgomery, Alabama, and the second one in the state. I still avoid confrontation with the press whenever it is possible if there is a controversial issue involving me.

When the head of the agency, Marshal James McShane, contacted me, he told me that Judge Johnson had recommended me highly. At the time I had not met Judge Johnson so I figured the background check the agents had done on me were the basis for his recommendation. It is normal procedure for anyone being employed on a government job to have this type of investigation, which included a criminal record check. Convictions for minor traffic offenses were not listed on such investigations unless they were excessive, but all other convictions were listed. Naturally convictions would count against anyone applying for a position in law enforcement.

I reported for duty as directed and was immediately taken

in by the chief deputy for an interview. His first statement concerned what had been written in the newspaper about the deputy who resigned after hearing of my being hired.

"I've done my research," he said, "and I know you're a good man. The United States Marshal's Office has no objection to your being hired except for one thing."

"What's that?" I asked.

"You were hired over the person that we had recommended," he said.

"Look," I said, "I do not wish to cause trouble between this office and Washington. I left my teaching job with the understanding that if things do not work out, I can return. Besides, as I see it, a veteran should be selected over a non-veteran, and a veteran with law enforcement background should be selected over one without a law enforcement background. A veteran with a law enforcement background and a college degree should be selected over one without the degree. I am a veteran with a law enforcement background and a college degree. Did the person you want to hire have all that?"

"No, he didn't have a college degree," he said.

"It's important for me to feel that I am fully qualified for this position. I do not want anyone giving me something because my face is black. But based on the government's selection criteria, I think I'm your man."

I was ready to return to the Montgomery County Board of Education and ask for my teaching job back if I saw any evidence that I was hired just to fill black quotas rather than because I was qualified for the job. I felt what James Brown said in one of his famous songs, "I don't want nobody to give me nothing, but open up the door and I'll get mine." I knew I could get mine if the door were opened.

The very first day of work turned out to be very interesting. We were told by the chief deputy during our orientation that the marshals had to keep a daily log, and we were shown how they should be made. The more I learned about the marshal's job the more interesting it seemed. We were informed that we would have to be prepared to take out of town trips, and perhaps we should get major credit cards else we would have to have cash for hotel rooms and meals while on such trips. We were also told that if such trips were for transporting prisoners, we would also need money for prisoners' meals if we were in charge of the trip. The job was really beginning to sound glamorous to me at this point. We were also told that on such trips, it might be necessary to hire an off-duty law enforcement officer to go along as a prison guard. If the trip were to last a week or more, it might not be possible to get an off-duty officer. In such a case, we could have a friend serve in that capacity. The friend would not have to be able to carry firearms. We were told the pay for the person hired and the amount that the government would pay for their food and lodging.

It wasn't very long before we were actually going on glamorous trips with experienced deputies as part of our training. We rode with them a few times while serving subpoenas, summons, complaints, and warrants of arrest. The training we received was mostly at the courtesy of the agency and deputies. Within a few days in the U.S. Marshals Office, I found myself on a trip to Petersburg, Virginia, with an experienced deputy. This was the best thing that could have ever happened for race relations in the United States Marshals Office in the Middle District of Alabama. Maybe even the whole federal building. Please note that all of these things were occurring just as the walls of segregation were being broken down. The older deputy was very concerned as to how the two of us would be received at hotels and restaurants while we were on this trip. Thrown together for several days, I expressed my concerns and feelings.

"I understand the frustrations of some whites," I told him. "I know there is going to be some resentment. I'll do what I can to make things easier."

"The head man at the office assigned us to take this trip together," he said. "I think he's expecting we're going to have some trouble on the trip."

I could tell my partner/instructor had some mixed feelings about our being assigned together so soon. Yet, he wanted to make me feel comfortable about being with him. He said, "I've been around Negroes all my life, and I've never had any trouble getting along with them."

"I've been around whites, too," I said, "but that relationship is different than ours will be."

In all my associations in the past, the white person was Mr. or Mrs. X and I was Arthur George. He had insisted earlier that I call him by his first name. I told him that that may go well on this trip, but depending on where we were, I would still call him Mr. X sometimes.

"What will your neighbors think," I asked him to consider, "if I walk up to you downtown one day and call you by your first name? Your neighbor's going to want to know 'Who is that nigger calling you by your first name?' and when you tell him 'We work together in the Marshal's Office,' it may be a put-down for you in the eyes of your neighbor."

I told him I did not come to integrate the U.S. Marshal's Office and that I did not intend to go tracking behind him at lunchtime. I did not want to make it uncomfortable for him when it came to his neighbors who may not have the same racial feelings as he had.

Upon returning to the office after this trip, Deputy X apparently told the rest of the staff the attitude I exhibited in our conversations while on the trip. Within a few days, everybody in the whole office was most cordial in attitude toward me. Everyone seemed a bit more comfortable in my presence. This included the secretaries in particular. The transition from the old way to the new way was very smooth and much of the smoothness could be attributed to the way I reacted to normal occurrences. I have always tried to see the other person's side of the issue or problem. For example, I tried to think why the U.S. Marshal's Office wanted to hire the other person instead of me. The other person had been available to the office for observation. He had, no doubt, gone on prison trips with some of the deputies. They knew about his law enforcement background because he worked in a supervisory position with the police department. They probably thought, *Arthur G. Worthy may be a good man, but our choice of hire is functional. We need someone who is functional.* To me, this is a reasonable, administrative decision. I later learned that there were some ill feelings between the deputy who had been assigned to carry me on my first trip and the head of the office. I felt an obligation to those who had supported my being hired, and I was determined not to let them down. That's the attitude that I had had ten years before when I had helped integrate the Montgomery Police Department. Going in with a chip on my shoulder would have been a destructive gesture. I took the attitude that no one actually had anything against Arthur G. Worthy just because I happened to be black, and I feel this attitude facilitated a smooth transition in the whole matter. Sometimes later, my North Carolina red-bone wife accompanied me and a female prisoner to the office, where my wife was observed by a number of white staffers in the building.

A day or so after the visit, a white female clerical worker said to me, "Now I understand why these white women don't excite you. I saw your wife the other day, and she is beautiful." I thought to myself *to you the fact that she looks white makes her beautiful.*

The duties of the Deputy U.S. Marshal would blow the mind of the average person. Often the U.S. Marshal is called in when jurisdiction is questioned. When civilians staged anti-war demonstrations on military bases around the country during the Vietnam crisis, military police had no authority to arrest the trespassers. The U.S. Marshal was the only law enforcement agent that had the authority to make the arrests. In some instances only a U.S. Marshal can arrest those violating laws outside of the territorial limits of the country. In other words, we could arrest anyone anywhere who hijacked an airplane as long as that airplane was licensed in the United States.

I went on many prison transportation trips or "PC trips" as we called them. These prisoner coordination trips became more and more interesting during the mid-sixties when racial segregation was still in effect in the South. Many eyes were opened both North and South when people saw a black Deputy Marshal transporting white prisoners. The fact that Deputy Marshals wore no uniforms made it even more confusing. I accepted the difficulty and inevitability of these trips because I knew what the office administrators were thinking: *If we make the wrong move we will be in court before Judge Johnson on a charge brought by the NAACP for discrimination against this colored deputy, and we probably won't have any support from headquarters because headquarters started this mess.* I felt sympathetic with those in charge of our operations. The general public does not realize the frustrations that many of these integration moves brought. The administrators had to appease all. You may ask, "How in the world did a little country boy from Marengo County, Alabama, become so open-minded and knowledgeable about the facts of life?" The answer: "It is a God-given blessing. When you hear some of the tribulations He brought me through, you will understand."

Very early in my employment, I found myself assigned as Deputy-In-Charge during a PC. Ironically, the other new deputy, who was white, went along as prison guard on this trip. It was a one-day trip, and after we returned we were told to report to the United States prison at Terre Haute, Indiana, for our U.S. Marshal training. I had a 1962 Chevrolet Bel-Aire which had no air conditioning, so we drove up in the other deputy's air-conditioned car. The training went well. I passed the firing test with the rating of marksman. The other deputy was excellent with a hand gun, and I believe he qualified with either expert or sharp shooter. Through years of employment, he always rated the highest score of anyone on the mandatory annual handgun qualifying.

The U.S. Marshal Service turned out to be such unusual work that I questioned the term *work*, particularly in the beginning. Sometimes I spent as many as four hours a day on stand-by. I had to show those four hours in my daily log of activities. It often seemed like a waste of time, and I was a bit self-conscious about putting those hours in the log. I later came to understand that this is common among higher-ups in the federal government. There was never any criticism from a supervisor. Within a year's period of my employment, incidents of national importance began to happen. One of the most notable was the Selma-to-Montgomery March protesting voting discrimination. The protesters' collision with local and state law enforcement on Bloody Sunday is no doubt what got the Feds involved. The marchers filed a civil action in the United States District Court in Montgomery against the Alabama Highway Patrol, the Dallas County Sheriff's Department, and the Selma Police Department so that they could participate in another protest march. The Federal Court issued an order to the marchers demanding that they wait until the Court could hear the facts.

Black extremists leaders became involved. They said, "We are marching Monday!" I was given a copy of the order to the marchers to serve on Ralph David Abernathy. Abernathy's aim was to not let the Black Panther leader take control of the movement. When I arrived in Selma, I found local law enforcement officers of every description as well as demonstrators of every description. There were white sympathizers, many from the North. I went to the Edmund Pettus Bridge that leads east toward Montgomery on U.S. Highway 80. The marchers had been stopped at the first traffic light just at the bridge. I was on the Selma side when I approached an officer of the State Highway Patrol. I showed him my Deputy Marshal's Identification and told him of the court order I needed to serve on Abernathy. I told him I wanted him to know who I was because I would be walking across the bridge to the traffic light. He was the highest ranking officer I saw,

and he immediately stopped another officer directing traffic
and instructed him to take me across the bridge, telling that
officer who I was. When I got to the other traffic light where
the marchers had been stopped, some of them told me that
Abernathy was at the church back in Selma. I began walking
toward the bridge where I had left my car. The demonstrators
were on the north side of the highway and the law enforcement officers were on the south side.

I had chosen to walk back on the side of the law enforcement officers and had gone past about two hundred and fifty
of them when one officer jumped in front of me saying, "Get
on over there with them!" All of the other officers seemed to
have known who I was but this officer. Before I could
respond, except to tell him, "I'm not with them," one of the
officers from before drove up in a state trooper's car and said,
"Marshal, I'll give you a ride to your car." I got in the Highway
Patrol car and left the officer with a foolish expression on his
face. He said something like, "I didn't know."

The church that I was supposed to go to was Brown
Chapel A.M.E. Zion. All I could think about was *why not a
Baptist church? Both King and Abernathy are Baptist ministers.*
The church was surrounded by law enforcement officers. I
approached a patrol captain and told him what my mission
was. He immediately offered to have some officers accompany
me into the church. I told him I would be safer alone, that if
accompanied by uniformed officers, we would have to fight
our way in and out. Upon learning that I was there, Rev.
Abernathy floor-showed me. He brought me to the front of
the church and told me what a good person I was.

"To show how good I know him to be," Rev. Abernathy
said, "I made him a deacon when I was his pastor, and he still

serves in the position." He made a big production of accepting the court order. He said to the group, "We are going to obey this order. We can wait." On the way out of the front door, I heard some mumbling from some of the extremists, but no one physically confronted me.

Within a few days, the court ordered the march without any interference from the state or local governing bodies. Deputy U.S. Marshals were called in from as far away as New York. The deputies had to accompany the marchers during the day and wherever they stopped for the night. The places they camped for the three nights are now marked as historical sites. My job was to protect the marchers as they slept in tents at night. The march ended at the state Capitol building on the fourth day with a series of speakers. When nothing happened at the sleeping tents during the three day march, I thought all was clear. I was very wrong.

The demonstrators were given rides by many of the sympathizers. One of those sympathizers, Viola Liuzzo, a white woman from Michigan, was shot and killed in Lowndes County. The killer, a white male, was quickly arrested and charged with murder. It was generally thought that he would not be found guilty because it was and is the procedure in criminal court to let the defense lawyer exclude anyone from jury service who might be prejudiced against the defendant. There were few black jurors in Lowndes County, and it could be reasonably assumed that any black person would be prejudiced in this case. Any black juror would automatically be excluded. He was, in fact, found not guilty at trial; however, in anticipation of this verdict, the federal prosecutors had also indicted him on federal civil rights violation charges. He was tried and convicted of violating the civil rights of Viola Liuzzo in the United States District Court for the Middle District of Alabama.

The convicted federal prisoner was in custody just long enough for the other prisoners to learn about his crime. I found myself with Collie Leroy Wilkins, the convicted killer of the now world-famous Liuzzo, whose death was considered a sacrifice to the cause of human rights. I took custody of him at the U.S. penitentiary at Atlanta, Georgia. We had a stop-over in Oxford, Mississippi, on our way to Terre Haute, Indiana. One of the black prisoners who had accompanied us from Atlanta expressed hostility toward Liuzzo's killer, and I became so concerned for Wilkins's safety, I asked the jail supervisor at Oxford to keep Wilkins separated from the other prisoners. I explained to the jailer that the hostility might come from some others as well since his victim had been a white woman.

"I don't want a dead body tomorrow," I told the supervisor. The whole experience was a bit unnerving. Since I was black, some people might assume I sympathized with the civil rights movement and think that I would help get back at Wilkins for his killing Liuzzo. But, as always, it was important to me not to take advantage of my law enforcement position. I delivered Wilkins to the penitentiary safely. "Thank you, God," I said upon getting a receipt for Collie Leroy Wilkins.

Arthur G. Worthy in his Army uniform.

No original exists of this photo from an old newspaper clipping announcing the May 3, 1954, hiring of Montgomery's first black policemen. The newspaper identified them as, from left, A. G. Worthy, W. L. Jarrett, and C. L. Prather. A fourth black officer and three black female school crossing guards were depicted (below) in a later article. From left, L. E. Jarrett, Arthur G. Worthy, Willie C. Miller, and Walter Lee Jarrett. The women are Jimmy Walton, Aileen Thornton, and Mary C. Johnson.

Above, Worthy as a U.S. Deputy Marshal on special
assignment overseeing the transport of nerve gas.
Below, Worthy with the BPOE (Elks) basketball team
which he coached and supported.

Arthur and Mildred Worthy, in a photo taken at
Community Congregational United Church of Christ.

Director's EEO Award presented to Arthur Worthy by the
Department of Justice.

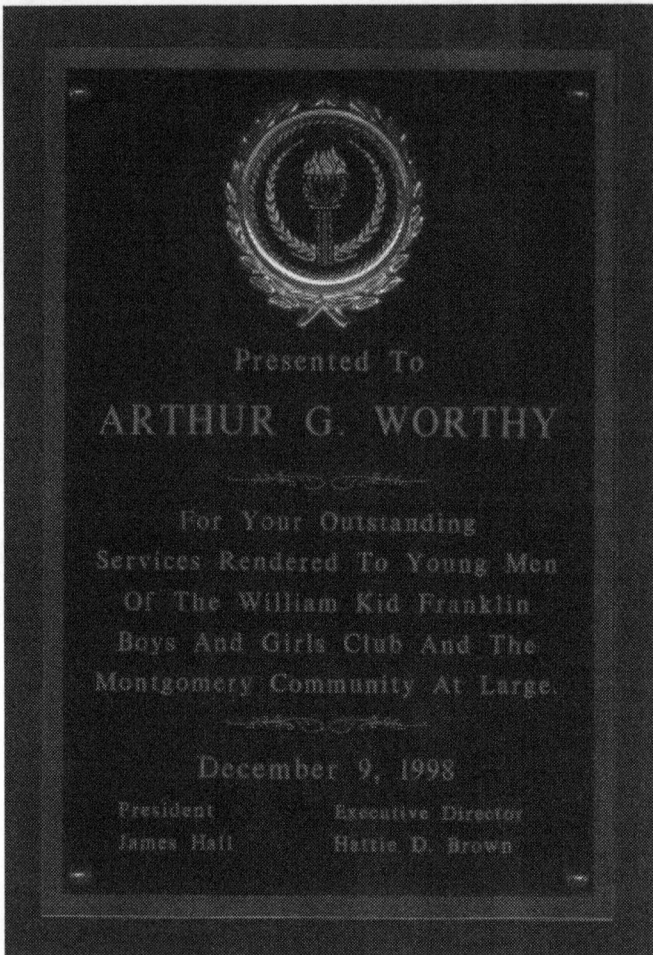

Award presented to Arthur Worthy by the William Kid
Franklin Boys and Girls Club.

# III

# USMS ASSIGNMENTS
# AND HISTORICAL EVENTS

RYING TO DECIDE which special assignments are most worthy of being mentioned is quite a task. Some of my United States Marshal Service (USMS) assignments sound like fiction written for movies or television. Being the only person from Alabama to be assigned as an instructor to the United States Treasury Law Enforcement Training Center was very important to me. Of course, this assignment did not get national attention like the trial of the world-famous prize fighter Marcellus Cassius Clay (Muhammed Ali) who was tried in the United States District Court at Houston, Texas, for failure to submit to the draft. His trial took place during a time in which anti-government sentiment was popular and there were protests nationwide against the Vietnam War. I was also assigned to the controversial trial of H. "Rap" Brown, head of the Student Nonviolent Coordinating Committee (SNCC), an organization made up mostly of black college students from the southeastern United States, then a hotbed of segregation. There were other nationally organized groups such as Sit-Inners, who wanted to integrate Southern lunch counters. Similarly the Freedom

Riders' mission was to integrate public transportation, particularly the Greyhound and Trailways buses as well as trains.

In law enforcement circles these groups were often called
hippies. The term *hippies* came from their far-out way of
dressing and the old expression, "I'm hip," which simply
means I know the real truth regardless of what you say. "Being
hip," "Having one's boots on," and "I know what time it is"
are expressions that originated in the black community and all
mean *I know the real truth.* It is important to emphasize that
the Freedom Riders and the Sit-Inners were integrated, usually made up of black college students and Northern white
sympathizers. Many of the famous incidents having to do
with the freedom riders and such groups occurred before I
became a deputy, but perhaps had some bearing on my being
hired and on James Meredith's integration of the University
of Mississippi. I still think Judge Frank M. Johnson, Jr., is
owed the biggest credit for my being employed, though.
Although my affiliation with Martin Luther King, Jr., was as
a law enforcement officer, I was very much respected by both
him and Ralph Abernathy, with whom I had had earlier
relationships. Ralph and I were teammates on the Linden
Academy High School basketball team, and he was my pastor
and I his deacon at First Baptist Church in Montgomery.

My assignments in the USMS were so numerous it is
impossible to name them all, but I do not want to give the
impression that my assignments were only in conjunction
with protesters. Protests were only a part of vast activities.
However, whenever there was a protest of national importance United States Marshals were called in. About the only
one of great significance that I was not involved in was the
American Indian protest at Wounded Knee, South Dakota. I

was not assigned to this operation as a peacekeeper because at the time I was detailed to the United States Treasury Law Enforcement Training Center as an instructor, and instructors were exempted from all special assignments. I became as familiar with the northeast United States, from Baltimore, Maryland, to Boston, Massachusetts, as I was with the twenty-three counties of the middle district of Alabama.

One of my most notable assignments was Project Watts at Camp Roberts, California. The name was designated by the then-Attorney General of the United States. To students of history who are meticulous enough to seek details, Watts was a predominantly black subdivision of Los Angeles, California. In 1965, the Watts Riot occurred. Historians like Della Rossa in her *Why Watts Exploded: How the Ghetto Fought Back* write about the causes, but since these are the memoirs of Arthur Worthy who is not a historian, I am not going to address *why* but *what* happened in Watts while I was there.

Deputies from Nebraska, California, Kansas, and I were assigned to Watts after the riots, along with two federal probation officers from Los Angeles and two border patrol officers. I do not mention names because I do not wish to be prosecuted in civil court for name defamation. Anyway, many of those being mentioned have passed on to their great reward. While on this assignment we did everything from escorting youth to social events to taking them fishing. Social workers were provided to work with the children all of the time. Whenever one of the children would get out of line, they would not hesitate to call us, "the enforcers," to take charge. I cannot recall ever taking any of the youth into custody. This would have come across as the federal government's being oppressive. After all, these were the underprivileged that had been taken advantage of by the local government. At least, that is how people nationwide seemed to think of them. There are those who will disagree with this point. Della Rossa's book, though, supports the idea. She mentions that Governor Brown appointed the McCone Commission to investigate "The Watts Problem."

According to Rossa the commission met more than three months, costing taxpayers $250,000, but brought no answers. I think any governor-appointed commission will have political overtones. Who would want it said that the governor did nothing? The suggestion that the commission did nothing is a political overtone. I am sure that there are probably hundreds of people whose opinions differ from mine. I respect such opinions as each person has a right to whatever opinion he or she may have. At the time I wondered why the U.S. Magistrate was not assigned to work Project Watts, but as I said before, the U.S. government did not want to be perceived as an oppressor as the local government had been. To assign a federal judge would have been going a step too far. I could just imagine the media blowing the whole matter out of proportion as usual. Given these statements and the statement made before regarding my avoiding the media, I may seem to be anti-press. Like politicians and religious leaders, the press plays on the emotions of the public for attention because it is easier to appeal to emotions than to reason and common sense. I do not like this even though I know it is necessary. Headlines blow facts out of proportion, and I have tried to avoid being part of the headlines.

At the end of the Watts assignment, we were complimented by the Attorney General of the United States for a job well done. The marshal from southern California became the

Director of the U.S. Marshals Service and was assigned to headquarters in Washington, D. C. The deputy from Maryland became Chief Deputy. The Assistant U.S. Attorney from Los Angeles was promoted to Assistant U.S. Attorney General. I was sent to the Treasury Law Enforcement Training Center. It seemed to me over the years that everyone in the service got more out of being assigned to Project Watts than I did.

After Los Angeles, my next significant assignment was the anti-war demonstration at the Pentagon. U.S. Deputy Marshals were called from all over the United States. Some districts were not able to respond to the call for help if they had too many other obligations like court appearances or prisoner transport activities. Some districts sent two deputies. Another deputy from Montgomery went along with me. Most of the deputies were assigned to stay in a hotel in Arlington, Virginia, that was not far from the Pentagon. The deputies met with the Assistant United States Attorney General the day before the demonstrations. He told us what to do and what to expect. We reported to the Pentagon the next morning as we had been instructed. The next eighteen hours were pure hell. We fought the demonstrators until some of the U.S. Department of Justice officials decided that the protests had gone far enough. They ordered us to arrest anyone who refused to vacate the property or who assaulted any officer. We were told where to secure those taken into custody and that we should be prepared to take them before the U.S. magistrates. After having made a number of arrests, I learned that a few FBI agents had stood around in suits and ties taking notes but had not gotten physically involved. I also learned that there had been 15,000 troops standing at parade rest in the Pentagon, out of sight of the media, while we were literally fighting like hell with demonstrators for eighteen hours without any relief. Here again, the government restrained troops because it did not want the press to picture the United States as an oppressor of free speech. Cameras were everywhere. Every time a Deputy U.S. Marshal would draw back his night stick, the camera would be right there to take a picture of the action.

I was out holding-the-line while facing the demonstrators and one of the black women protestors asked, "Are you what they call an Uncle Tom?" She was attempting to embarrass me and make me feel bad for protecting government property.

"No, ma'am," I responded, "I'm Uncle Tom's nephew and a different breed."

I had experienced this type of ill-feeling many years earlier as a city police officer. In the black community there was a feeling that all law enforcement officers were anti-black. That's why, as I stated earlier, Dr. Walton had said it was difficult to get black men to apply when the city of Montgomery decided to hire black police officers. It was generally felt in the black community that anyone who took a job in law enforcement was just being used by the white controllers to suppress the rights of poor colored people.

After the anti-war demonstrations, I had no assignments of great national significance until February 16, 1968. At this time I was called to Buffalo, New York, in the matter of *USA v. Thomas Carrela* in the United States District Court for West New York. Carrela was an alleged member of the Mafia. My duties in this assignment were to protect the witness who happened to be a federal prisoner already serving a sentence. It is during this time I learned that there were officers of the law who could not be trusted.

While waiting to testify, the government witness had to be housed in a room in the federal building that had been set up as a bedroom. Even though the local jails contracted with the federal government to house federal prisoners, the government was afraid to put him in any local jail because the Mafia was believed to have contacts within law enforcement. Thomas Carrela was such a big family member the witness who testified against him would not have had a chance in a local jail.

This blew my mind. Down South, an officer could always trust another officer regardless of jurisdiction. I said to myself, *Wake up, Arthur George. You ain't down home no more.* The witness insisted we play penny poker, and at night when my shift worked, we would play. At least the game kept the twelve-hour shift from being too boring. The assignment lasted about ten days. That was the practice. A deputy would stay on an assignment ten days, and if it lasted longer, new deputies would come in and the old deputies would return to their assigned districts.

I was not lucky to have a short assignment the next time. The Black Panthers, whose home base was in California, made a threat against U.S. District Judge James B. Parsons. Judge Parsons was a black federal judge assigned to Chicago. You might wonder, "Why would the Black Panthers threaten the life of a black federal judge?" I can only say it was the times we were living in. This assignment began for me on October 16, 1968, and lasted until November 27, the day before Thanksgiving. A judge must rule within the law whether or not individuals trespass on government property. Either the individuals had business on the property or they did not have business on the property. The Black Panthers took the position that if the judge himself is black, he should not rule against his own people regardless of the facts of the case. To me, this type of thinking reflects the illogic of these extremist groups and how they appealed to their followers' emotions rather than their reason and common sense.

The judge became attached to me to the extent that he refused to let me be relieved to return to my assigned district at the scheduled time. One day I told him that my wedding anniversary was coming up on November 11, and he told me to have Mildred come to Chicago. He said we could go with him to his lake home at Benton Harbor, Michigan, right on Lake Michigan. Mildred came to Chicago, and we had a ball that weekend at Judge Parsons's home. When I said that Judge Parsons became attached to me that was not the whole truth. He had, in fact, become attached to the whole group of deputies who were first sent, and he did not want to get adjusted to a group of new personalities.

After all, these new men would be coming from all over the United States and perhaps some of the territorial districts such as Guam or Puerto Rico. There might be language barriers. He felt *I've got a good group here and I'm going to insist on keeping them.* On one occasion the judge was invited to speak at the annual Patent Lawyers' Association meeting. Two of us went along to protect him. This meeting turned out to be quite interesting in that it taught me something about lawyers' areas of specialization. I knew of specializations such as criminal or civil law, but patent law? I had never even thought about it.

Whenever the judge would decide to go to his lakeside home on weekends, he would take only two deputies because whoever went with him had to stay in the lake home. There were no motels or hotels in the immediate vicinity. When the local marshal learned that there were sometimes two deputies standing by at the hotel on weekends, he started requesting that we accompany the local deputy on short overnight PC trips to Sandstone, Minnesota. I went one weekend.

Finally November 27 arrived and I headed home. I thought this would be the easy part, but the day I departed I encountered more traffic than I have ever seen in my life. The traffic was so slow it took us four hours to make it to the airport. Even though my flight was at 1:00 p.m. and I could see the airport just ahead by 1:30 p.m., we didn't actually make it to the airport until 2:30 p.m., one hour too late. I couldn't get another flight until the next day, Thanksgiving. I stayed at a hotel close by, and finally made it home to Mildred, happy but too late for the traditional Alabama State versus Tuskegee Thanksgiving Day game.

Following Judge Parsons's Chicago assignment, the northern assignments became too numerous to list. I do not understand why those of us from the southern districts always seemed to get the Mafia-related crime assignments. Whether it was a court appearance, judge protection, or witness protection, we Southern boys were called. I think that the Service was probably afraid to overexpose local deputies in these high profile cases. I was told by a few friends in the northeastern districts that they were approached with money. One deputy said he was asked what his pay was and when he answered, he was told, "That's just chicken feed. I can give you three times that." This type of occurrence frightened me.

So many assignments stand out in my mind. I protected foreign dignitaries at the United Nations General Assembly in

New York, one of my most interesting assignments. The first dignitary I worked with was Lord Carrington, the British Foreign Minister from England. I must mention here that *Lord* is a title in Britain like *Mr.* is a title in this country. The difference is *Lord* is inherited from being born into certain families. Lord Carrington had been assigned his own airplane by the British government. He knew more people in New York than I did. He also had English bodyguards. He appeared on the morning television show, "Good Morning, America," and we had to accompany him as his security. At one time we were supposed to fly with him to the West Coast, but something happened and the trip was canceled. We did go with him to Washington, D.C., on his plane. It was my first time landing at that particular airport in Virginia.

While on this assignment, there was a code name for all of the places that an assigned deputy might have to go. The John F. Kennedy Airport was *Strategic*, the LaGuardia Airport was *Big Ben*, The Newark Airport was *By-Pass*, The United Nations Headquarters was *Alamo*, the U.S. Marshal was *Crockett*, The Waldorf Astoria Hotel was *Palace*, The U.N. Plaza Hotel was *Texas*, and the Summit Command Post was *Summit*. If we went to any of these places, we communicated by radio and we had to use the code names. After a week or two, Lord Carrington had to return to England on some kind of emergency. During the time I was with him, I became friendly with his Scotland Yard agents. Years later when I was vacationing in England, I made contact with one of them. There was no real language barrier though some people say that British people are speaking a foreign language because they pronounce words so differently. Some British people say we in the United States speak American, not English. Those deputies who had been working with Lord Carrington were told that we could return to our assigned districts. On the morning I was to leave for Montgomery, the supervisor came to my room and told me to report to Summit for a new assignment.

My new assignment was the Iraq Foreign Minister. Iraq and Iran had just gone to war with each other two weeks before. For the first time I felt that anywhere we escorted him, everyone would be blown away. Luckily for us, things went smoothly. Unlike Lord Carrington, the Iraq minister would go to United Nations Headquarters for meetings and then back to the hotel where he always had his meals in the hotel. He did not appear on "Good Morning, America," much to my personal satisfaction. He kept close to his hotel when he was not attending a United Nations session. I do not know what became of the Iraq Foreign Minister, but in 2000, I learned from a British couple vacationing here in the Smoky Mountains that Lord Carrington was still alive.

I worked in Operation CHASE, helping the U.S. Military remove nerve gas used in the war. When anti-war demonstrations began to grow, the military decided to take nerve gas from various locations around the country, ship it on freight trains, transport it to the ocean, load it on barges, pull the barges out, and sink them to a destructive depth. When the military made known its plan to transport the material through various cities and counties, many sheriffs and police chiefs put the word out: "If they bring that dangerous material through my jurisdiction, I'm going to arrest them." With this threat, the military obtained a court order that prohibited interference with movement of these materials. The federal court order automatically brought in the United States Marshal Service. I was not just assigned to Operation CHASE. I was the USMS In Charge of Operations. From Fort McClelland, Alabama, to Sunny Port, North Carolina, things went well. Even though we got word that there would be a student demonstration at Athens, Georgia, there was no incident.

Sometime in early 1971, there came an order for refresher training of U.S. Deputy Marshals. I took the first class scheduled and received the highest scholastic award. Receiving that award, I very much impressed Inspector James A. Gardner who always found a way to make sure I was considered for all assignments of national significance. I never got to thank him, and I now feel guilty about that. It was he who put me in charge of Operation CHASE. Inspector Gardner had confidence in my ability, and I tried never to let him down by messing up an assignment he gave me.

As a result of my award, I was chosen to attend Treasury Law Enforcement School in the early part of 1972. This class had seven women—Phyllis Frances Shantz and Kathryn I. Clark, of Washington, D.C.; Sara Elizabeth Durant-Milton, Massachusetts; Janet P. Ingram, Colorado Springs; Susan Gail Rowley, Hialeah, Florida; and Phyllis A. Barrett, New Orleans—the first women agents hired by the U.S. Customs Service and the U.S. Immigration Service. No doubt the government had seen the handwriting on the wall. It was just a matter of time before American women demanded employment rights in all areas. Although I did not have the highest average for this school, I did well. I made 824 out of a possible 1000. The class average was 885. The minimum passing score was 750.

Politicians started complaining about all the governmental training schools. Someone came up with the idea of consolidating all federal law enforcement. All agencies went along with the idea except the FBI whose director at the time was J. Edgar Hoover. He felt it would be demeaning to his agency to be classed with other federal agents. Congress began to pressure Mr. Hoover to comply with the idea. However, when the pressure became strong, Mr. Hoover began to non-publicly let various persistent Congressmen and Senators know of his secret files on their wrongdoings. He knew of laws they had broken, and he let it be known that he would make public those files. They immediately backed off. All the public knows is that the FBI did not become a part of the Consolidated Federal Law Enforcement Training Center. These statements are Arthur Worthy's version of what happened. No one really knows what happened. If they do, they are not talking. Anyone who might know is either dead, or, like me, has reached the age of senility.

Less than a year after finishing U.S. Treasury School, I was assigned as an instructor when it became part of the Consolidated Federal Law Enforcement Training Center. Upon arrival in Washington, D.C., we were required to take a short instructor's training course. The instructor was an employee of the U.S. Department of the Treasury. Upon learning of my degree in education and my eight-year teaching experience, I was frequently called upon when there was a problem, real or imagined. We were asked to rewrite one or two of the courses being taught in the police school. The assignment was supposed to last ten months, but it ended earlier for me.

I worked all sorts of other details. I worked in Miami, Florida, during a labor dispute between a small shipping dock operator and the labor union, which represented the dock workers. Merchant Marines, they were called. On one occasion I worked this assignment nearly three weeks. We would pick up the operator from his residence in the morning and take him to the shipping docks. Joey Titlebaum turned out to be a very interesting character. I can remember taking him deep-sea fishing a time or two. I thought about the possibility of someone shooting us with a high-powered rifle while we were at sea. We were in his boat and the dock workers must have known what it looked like. Titlebaum would not go anywhere without his bodyguards. When he was at home, he had someone watch his residence. Titlebaum demanded, however, that no female deputies be assigned to protect him. On one occasion when I was working as a supervisor, a female deputy from Kentucky was put on his detail. Learning that a woman had been assigned, he became very upset over the idea that his safety was of such little importance in the eyes of the federal government. We were in a bind. We could not send the woman back to her district. To solve the problem, we assigned her to his residence at night when he did not know who was there.

The detail lasted some two years. The last time I worked it, I had made inspector. When the supervisor learned of my promotion, I was assigned to the office for ten days to answer the phone. I never realized how boring this job could be. He made the assignment out of respect for my new grade, but I saw the activity as demeaning.

# IV

# EEO MEMOIRS & HOBBIES

I N THE BEGINNING of the United States Marshal Service, the term EEO (Equal Employment Opportunity) had no service-connected meaning. All EEO functions were performed by the Equal Employment Opportunity Commission, a separate agency in the federal government. A complaint of discrimination was reported directly to the commission, and any investigation or counseling was done by the commission. At some point, the government began having the various departments develop their own EEO programs. I took a course on human relations at the police academy in Memphis, Tennessee. The course prepared me to work in EEO as either a counselor or investigator. I attribute my success in law enforcement to my human relations skills.

Whenever the word discrimination is heard, everyone thinks black, female, or over forty. Even lawyers are reluctant to take a complaint that does not involve the aforementioned groups. I gained national attention when I was brought in as an EEO counselor on behalf of a white male. No one thought a white man could be discriminated against. It seemed that the

Civil Rights Act of 1964 was seldom scrutinized or read closely by those in the business.

After the various governmental agencies became involved in processing complaints of discrimination, it was still the policy to involve EEOC only when a complaint could not be resolved at the local level. State and local agencies were ordered by federal court to set up their own programs, usually after a Federal District Court ruled that these agencies had discriminated.

During the twenty years I served in the United States Marshal Service, I worked for agencies all over the United States including those other than the marshal service. Why was I the exception in being assigned cases outside my judicial district? I was known to be a successful counselor. The EEO Officer for the United States Marshal Service would assign me when the situation was complicated, like the class action complaint that accused the United States Marshal Service and the Department of Justice of under-staffing an all-black office to the point of danger. I counseled a number of complaints from Cuban Americans who thought they were discriminated against because of their national origin. I successfully negotiated a promotion on behalf of a white marshal from one of the Latin American countries who became an American citizen. He worked in one of the Border States and was hired primarily to deal with Spanish speakers.

I use no names in this portion since it is against the law to publicly name a person who receives EEO services. I received the shock of my life when I was getting ready to retire at 55 (the mandatory retirement age for deputies) after twenty years of service. I had copies of all the EEO reports I had made over that period of time. I knew that the files were confidential. I called the USMS EEO office and asked if they wanted me to send the files there. They told me to take the files home. I understand why when shortly after going home, people began to call me. I explained to them I was retired and they would have to use another counselor. They would just say, "Them folks don't know nothing." It seemed that everyone knew my nature: I cannot say no. The USMS EEO Office would frequently call inquiring about a case that I had counseled. I first considered it foolish and unnecessary to bring those records home with me, but it turned out to be very helpful. I even went back to testify in court twice.

In trying to get these memoirs ready for publication before my time on earth expires, I found a box of old EEO files. I had forgotten that some of these ever existed. I did not realize I had done so much EEO work in Washington, D.C. I knew that the class action complaint that listed the U.S. Department of Justice as one of the ADO's originated there, but there were numerous others. There are some who would associate the South with discrimination, but that is a misconception. New York, Michigan, Illinois, Ohio, Indiana, New Jersey, and other states above the Mason-Dixon Line have discrimination too. Speaking of the Mason-Dixon Line, I never experienced this, but I was told by some of my elders that if a black person were on a passenger train coming South and happened to be seated with white folks, when the train crossed the Mason-Dixon Line, the black person had to go to the back of the coach.

The business of EEO became of national significance after the passage of the Civil Rights Act of 1964. This act created the U.S. Civil Service Commission. In the beginning everyone associated EEO with federal employees. Now it applies to all state, federal, or private employees. Section 501 of the Act protected individuals with certain disabilities. The law is frequently misinterpreted. Some years after retirement when I became an EEO officer for the Montgomery Police Department, I had a case in which a man with an amputated leg applied for a job as a police patrolman. He was rejected because of the amputation. He thought he was protected by the Act. He filed a complaint with the EEOC at Birmingham. I had to get him straight.

The business of EEO counseling was one of my hobbies during my working years. My second hobby was handwriting analysis. I later became a master certified graphoanalyst. During the few months that I was an instructor at the Consolidated Federal Law Enforcement Training Center in D.C., I developed an interest in document examination. To me, the criminal investigator who could determine the origin of a document was at the top of the ladder in an investigation. Proficiency in these areas is mostly self-achieved through the study of various books on the subject. The art of revealing personality through handwriting is amazingly accurate. I still have dozens of books which I purchased in bookstores from New York to California.

I would engage hotel clerks in conversations about handwriting analysis. In most cases, the clerks would ask me to analyze their handwriting. After those who knew me considered me a handwriting expert, I saw an advertisement for Continuing Education in an eight-step handwriting analysis class at Troy State University at Montgomery. We were told after completing the class that we could enroll in a correspondence course offered by the International Graphoanalysis

Society in Chicago, Illinois. After finishing the course, we received a certificate of achievement that made my college degree look bad. I took the correspondence course which consisted of twenty assigned lessons. After studying and working through the assignments, many of which I completed in hotels across the country while on assignment as a marshal, I was issued a completion certificate.

Because of my outgoing personality, it became widely known that I was a handwriting expert. A deputy asked me, "What is it about you that everybody seems to be attracted to? Every city we go to people just come up to you."

"Handwriting analysis," I responded. "I've either analyzed their writing or they know someone whose handwriting I've analyzed."

"I see it's the women too," he said. "North or South, black or white."

"I engage them in conversation with the handwriting. Everyone's interested in that subject."

"If handwriting analysis is that interesting, I need to become involved in that," he said.

I don't know if he ever took up handwriting analysis. I know he did not take it up to the extent as yours truly, Art Worthy. Over the years I tried to improve my skills. I became a Master Graphoanalyst, and I taught the eight basic steps at two of the local universities. Eventually I became a member of the World Association of Document Examiners. I even offered testimony in court over a disputed will. Some sisters and brothers accused one of their brothers of changing their parents' will. The accused man went into the marshal's office in Birmingham and asked where he could find a handwriting expert. One of the deputies told him that the only handwriting expert he knew was in Montgomery, Alabama. He gave the man my telephone number and address, and the man called me the next day. He told me his parents had recently died and left him some property, but his brothers and sisters were accusing him of forging the parents' name on the will. He wanted to bring me some documents so that I could give him an expert opinion as to the legitimacy of the signatures. I told him that my opinion would be unofficial because I had not been recognized as an expert by any court, but that there was a man in Auburn the State of Alabama had used in questioned document cases. I gave him the man's name and phone number.

Two days later, the accused man called me back and said, "You can do this for me. Let me bring you the will and some other documents."

"Okay," I said, and I gave him the directions to my house. He brought me the papers.

"What will your charge be?" he asked.

"No charge," I said. "This is a hobby for me. I wouldn't feel right charging you."

I mailed him the report and forgot about it until about two weeks later when I got a telephone call from his lawyer. "I read the report that you did for my client and I think it is wonderful," the lawyer said.

"Thank you, sir," I said, feeling very pleased that I had done a good job.

"We want you to testify in court," he said.

"Of all the judges in the state of Alabama that know me, there is not a single one who would certify me an expert," I said.

"Mr. Worthy, that is not true," he said. "The judge read

your report and has already certified you as an expert."

I was floored. I told him that since I was now retired and uncommitted, I would testify if he sent me the notice. The day I went to court I was surprised to see the person in Auburn who did the work for the state of Alabama testifying for the other side. I was even more surprised when the judged ruled the man I was testifying for the winner. I was overjoyed that justice had been done and that the man was able to get what his parents had left him. The Court for Shelby County paid me witness fees and travel from Montgomery. The man could not accept my not charging him, and he delivered to me the most beautiful telephone I have ever seen. I still have it. Over the next two years, he recommended me to at least a dozen people. I found excuses to turn them all down. *Stick to your graphoanalysis, Art Worthy,* I told myself.

Some Alabama educators learned of my graphoanalysis and invited me to speak at various group meetings around the state. At each gathering I would be asked to analyze the handwriting of one or more of the people in attendance. Sometimes I would accompany my wife Mildred, who was the third from the top of the Alabama Education Association. When I was with her, she did not ask me to appear on programs. She felt that if she had, it would look like she planned it that way and that would not have been good for membership relations. About the only organization I worked with that had no interest in my graphoanalysis was the Elks Southern Pride Lodge #431. The Elks were interested in listening to music or looking for drinks.

While I was Exalted Ruler of my lodge, I took up a different hobby, coaching basketball. I organized a junior herd, the Junior Elks, who played very well city-wide.

we went to a big dinner party thrown for us in Morocco. Dancing girls surrounded me and played on my lap. I liked that dinner better than Mildred did.

We have traveled to Fiji, Aruba, St. Croix, St. Thomas, Hawaii and Puerto Rico, and many, many other exotic islands, but our favorite was Jamaica. The second time we went, I did not know we were going until we reached the airport. Mildred took me there as a surprise birthday present.

Even though my health will not allow us to travel any longer, we have many wonderful memories. You might ask how people of ordinary means accomplished something as extraordinary as seeing the world? I'll tell you. That was our choice. Mildred and I chose to spend our money on what was important to us and not to worry about how other people spent theirs. I am so glad I decided early in life that we would enjoy ourselves as we went along rather than waiting until retirement as so many others have.

# V

# SPIRITUALLY SPEAKING

WHILE I WAS POLICING, teaching, and marshaling, there was another side of my life that was more important. The side, in fact, that may have influenced all the other events. You might have figured out from some of my experiences that I am well acquainted with "the man upstairs," God. No one could have come through some of the experiences I have come through on his own. I have never met anyone I felt was all bad. Even the bank robbers who got the upper hand on my partner and me and handcuffed us to a tree in Western Kentucky on a cold February day had some good in them. We were able to persuade them to go to our car, get our overcoats, take off the handcuffs, put the overcoats on us before they re-cuffed us so we wouldn't freeze to death before someone found us. I am very sure it was God who brought me through that experience alive.

I haven't mentioned my spiritual life up until now? I can only tell you this is the way and the order in which I have chosen to write my memoirs. Those who know me accept the fact that whatever Arthur G. Worthy does—whether making an arrest, conducting equal employment opportunity counseling, or inspecting a county jail that has contracted to keep federal prisoners—will be done the Arthur Worthy way. I am not really bragging when I tell you my way has been accepted by whoever needs to give approval for the action, even if the action were baptizing an adult new member when the pastor of the church had a backache.

My spiritual/religious life has sometimes been as controversial as my everyday life. Just before leaving the Montgomery Police Department, where I worked for almost three years, we moved to the north side of town, and we changed our membership from Bethel Baptist Church to First Baptist Church, where Ralph David Abernathy was the pastor. Ralph and I had known each other since childhood. He was a few years older than I, but we played basketball together for Linden Academy in Linden, Alabama. I don't say the hometown team because he lived on a rural route to the north and I lived on a rural route ten miles south of Linden. Upon joining First Baptist, Abernathy began grooming me for the position of General Superintendent of the Sunday School. There was an older deacon who had held the position for a number of years, but he was just a little bit over-the-hill. The man had been very good at one time, but by the time I got there, he was just a little too old for the demands of the job. Further, he had a limited education and was not the man that Abernathy wanted to represent First Baptist before the National Baptist Convention, which had its origin at First Baptist Church. Abernathy wanted someone with at least as much training as most of his Sunday school teachers, who were, for the most part, teachers in the public school system.

They were all female, however. There were some high school principals among the members, but they all worked out of town. There was only one other man with a college degree who worked in the city. It was a little uncomfortable to realize that in the colored community, people who considered themselves anybody were members of Holt Street, Dexter Avenue, or First Baptist, if they were Baptist, and St. John A.M.E. or Old Ship A.M.E. Zion if they were Methodist. Ninety-nine percent of the professional people, teachers, lawyers, and doctors belonged to the churches mentioned. Attorney Fred Gray was an exception. He was Church of Christ.

I worked at the same school as some of the Sunday school teachers and thought I knew them very well until I was designated General Superintendent. Some of those old sisters thought I was the worst appointment possible: "It's the awfulest thing in the world! Designating this little nobody from down-in-the-country who did not grow up in First Baptist, has no family history, and, to add insult to injury, is a policeman when everybody knows there is no such thing as a good police." I know it is hard to believe, but some of the Sunday school teachers stopped speaking to me for a while after my appointment.

One of the most difficult things I have had to do was organize the Sunday school teachers' weekly meetings. After the attempted bombing of the church, all the Sunday school teachers had a ready-made excuse not to attend. There were one or two older teachers who claimed that they had no way to get to the meeting, but I resolved that by picking them up. Eventually, everything began to go smoothly. When I sort of got my feet under me, I started to rub it in with my name. I used to tell the Sunday school, "There are not many churches who are blessed enough to have a *Worthy* General Superintendent of its Sunday school." After I was ordained as deacon, I really emphasized both my names, *Arthur* and *Worthy*.

"If you look up the origin of the Old English word *Arthur*, you will find it means *noble*. Now, how can you beat having a *noble* Worthy deacon?" I would say. My sons thought it was comical, as I made everything, even their punishments. It did not go over well with my wife and daughter. The daughter soon accepted it as Daddy's way, and she saw I could make it inoffensive to the audience. Mildred never got that far. She thought it was awful to say something like that at a church gathering.

I never had any problems communicating with my children. The same thing was true at school. My students at school would accept whatever was done. I had a student tell me once, "Mr. Worthy, you hit much harder than the principal, but I'd ten times rather have you whip me than that principal."

"Boy, are you trying to tell me you love pain?" I asked.

"No, no," he said. "Every time you get ready to whip me you sit me down and talk to me and by the time you finish talking to me, I feel that if I didn't get that whipping, I would not live to see tomorrow." I thought this was very touching.

On another occasion, I was whipping a boy in class when the supervisor of instruction came in. The child jumped up and said, "I'm getting exactly what I deserve. Mr. Worthy is doing nothing wrong." The supervisor was so taken aback until she could not speak. She went back to the principal's office and told him what she had observed in my room.

"I've had the shock of my life," she said.

"Mr. Worthy has an unusual relationship with his students. No one really understands it. It's not strange to see him shooting marbles with the boys or playing hopscotch with the girls. He conducts his class discussions in the TV and radio quiz show style. The children love it," the principal explained.

For years to come she was still amazed and would frequently mention the incident to teachers' groups when she had the occasion to speak. She might not have known that one reason I enjoyed a good relationship with my students was I did not give homework. We did all work in class because I felt that any work done at home would be completed by the parents or not at all. The whole idea was unfair to those children of non-educated parents.

To get back to my own children, I had some experiences that are worth mentioning. One day Michael, the youngest child, came from school all excited. As we sat at the dinner table, we discussed what had happened that day. Michael yelled out, "Old Wallace did it!"

"Michael, son, Wallace didn't kill the President as you say," I explained.

"Yes, he did," Michael said. I could tell the topic had been discussed at school with some friends. Then the other two children Carol and Arthur Jr., chimed in with what Wallace had been saying in his speeches over the television. They had not actually been listening to Wallace's pro-segregation political speeches; they had been listening to anti-Wallace street talk, usual to black communities. I could not believe how anti-Wallace all three of our children were even though we had never expressed such hostile feelings in their presence. I said to myself, *I have got to get these children on the right foot in their thinking about life in general.*

"From now on," I told them, "when Wallace gives his

political speeches, we are going to sit down as a family and listen. When the speech is over, we will discuss what was said as a family. As your father, it is my duty to see that you make up your own minds as to whether or not you like George Wallace.

"If you do that," my oldest son, Arthur, Jr., said, "you will be the meanest daddy in the whole world."

"Look," I said, "I do not care if you like George Wallace or not. I want you to be able to make an intelligent decision and not base that decision on what someone else has said. Further, as a Christian, you are supposed to love everybody in spite of who they are."

In the months that followed I unintentionally made Arthur, Jr., one the biggest Wallace supporters. When voting time came, he suggested that we vote for Wallace or one of his proposals. I reminded him of how he thought I was the meanest daddy in the world for making him listen to the speeches.

"I know that you were trying to make us make up our own minds as to whether or not we disliked Wallace instead of listening to what others said about him," he said. He told me this right before he entered high school. I thought I had gotten my son Michael straight also, but as he became a teenager, I found out he had a serious problem I had never attempted to correct because I didn't know about it. He was a little dictator among his friends. The other parents in the neighborhood did not understand why Michael's peers would jump to his every command. I learned, one day, quite by accident, that he had been threatening that if they did not do what he said, he would not let them swim in our family's pool. When I learned this, I let the other children know that it was I who had to give approval, and that they were welcome as long as there was an adult at home if one of their parents were not with them. After that, Michael's peers began finding out how sensitive he was.

I did not realize how sensitive Michael was about what we owned until one day I was called by his junior high teacher and told Michael owed for several weeks school lunches. He was found out to be getting free lunches when he was supposed to be paying. When I questioned Michael about why he had not been paying for his lunches, he said, "All of my friends are in the free-lunch line, and I want to be with them."

I did not accept this as an excuse.

Finally he confessed, "Everybody teases me. They say, 'Michael's parents are rich. They live in a big, two-story house with a swimming pool and his mother is white.'"

I said to myself *Arthur George, you did not do the job you thought you did. You've got some work to do here.* After much discussion, I thought I got him to understand that as long as he showed sensitivity to what his peers said, they would continue to tease him.

"Michael," I said, "Your mother is not white, even if she does look like it." I realized later that I did not get over with my emphasis to him. This sensitivity followed him to adulthood.

When my daughter reached her teens in high school, I felt it was time to school her in the facts of life. During one of our conversations I said, "You are growing and there will be people making sexual advances toward you that may blow your mind. You might even be approached by a male teacher, if you haven't already, and I want you to be prepared. Men are not daddy figures. Be prepared to say 'no' in a very convincing way."

When she was approached, she said to the teacher, "Daddy told me I should expect this. I'm not offended but my answer is no. You've got the wrong girl."

The male teacher was so shocked at her response he said, "Your daddy has really educated you in the facts of life."

Some years later my daughter was enrolled as a freshman at Harvard. (She enrolled at Radcliffe College but during her freshman year, Radcliffe, which was for girls only and Harvard University, which was for boys only, merged and became Harvard University. Radcliffe College lost its identity. I'm getting historical again.) Anyway, my daughter was visited by a roommate from college. She had visited the roommate's home in Philadelphia for Thanksgiving and the roommate visited her for Christmas. The roommate thought visiting us was like looking at the television show *All in the Family* because we comfortably discussed everything. It was mind-blowing to her how openly we discussed sex.

In the years that followed I had some very rich spiritual experiences in First Baptist as well as the community in general. I spoke on a number of occasions and I was called to teach Sunday school classes at other churches for Men's Day, both in and out of town, and at various church anniversaries. While I was teaching, to help with heavy financial burdens, I also worked as a bouncer keeping order at a night club. I got the job because of my police experience.

One Saturday the minister came to me and said, "Brother Worthy, my back is hurting me and tomorrow is Baptismal Day. There are several adults to be baptized. Would you do the physical work for me while I perform the rituals?"

I told him I would be glad to do it, and the following day the very first person to be baptized was a young lady who had frequented the night club where I worked on weekends. I had just seen her there the night before. When she saw me, she whispered, "Not You!"

I just nodded my head and whispered, "It's all right," and submerged her under the water.

This particular member became active in church but did not stop attending the night club on weekends. She would frequently say to friends accompanying her, "He'll be at church bright and early tomorrow."

The minister knew of my weekend activities but never said once that I should not be doing them. In fact I was a bouncer under the administration of at least two different ministers. Everyone accepted the fact that Arthur G. Worthy had his head on straight. One of the night clubs I worked in was owned by one of the deacons of the famous Dexter Avenue Baptist Church. The night clubs were safe places since most of the patrons were professed Christians. There were no drive-by shootings in those days.

Stay with me: It was my spiritual connection which enabled me to deal with the racial problem effectively. In the first place, I did not take offense for what many persons would have been offended by. For example, during the years 1964–1965, the federal government, through the Department of Labor, started enforcing the minimum-wage law. There were a number of small businesses guilty of violating this law. I was given an injunction to serve on the operator of a small business that was located on Dexter Avenue. When I went to the business, I was told that the man I wanted to see had gone home, and I was given a home address on a street just south of the Southern Bypass. Upon ringing the doorbell, I was confronted by an occupant of the house, and I identified myself as being from the U.S. Marshal's Office.

"Are you Mr. X?" I asked the man who had appeared at the door with a drink in his hand.

"I am," he said.

"I am here to serve you with this injunction," I said. Instead of taking the papers, he threw the drink in my face.

"I'm leaving the papers," I said. I touched him with the papers. "You've been legally served." I dropped the papers at his feet. "You should contact a lawyer for advice."

When I returned to the office, I reported the incident to the U.S. Marshal. He immediately insisted that I make a report to the FBI and have them charge the man with assaulting a federal officer while in the performance of his duties. I told the marshal that action would only strain race relations even further. It would only bring me attention and the racial extremists would be looking for Arthur G. Worthy on every corner. This incident happened during the Selma-to-Montgomery March when marshals from all over the country were in town, even the Director of the Service. The Director agreed with me.

Another incident occurred some years later when I had been given a summons and complaint to serve on a white female who worked in one of the cotton mills in Lanett, Alabama. When I went into the mill manager's office, he looked at me with a mean expression and asked, "What do you want, boy?"

"Sir, I am from the U.S. Marshal's Office in Montgomery, and I have some papers for Mrs. X," I replied. By that time, the secretary felt a need to become involved in the matter. She saw the manager seemed very irritated by my presence, and she wanted to make sure that the boss did not put his foot in his mouth.

"Who did you say you were with?" she asked.

I pulled out my credentials—my badge and my identification.

"Yes, yes, she works here. I'll be glad to get her for you," she said.

She left her office and while she was gone, the manager became overly friendly. He began telling me about his having grown up in Montgomery in the Riverside Public Housing Project. Finally the secretary came back with the woman I was to serve the papers on. I did so and was about to leave when the manager began talking again. He did everything but apologize for his obvious initial displeasure with my presence.

"I understand your feelings. I am not offended," I said. "I was born in Alabama. Any white man born in Montgomery, Alabama, would have felt the same way you felt seeing a black man in a suit and tie walk in an ask to see a white, female employee." I could see I blew his mind. "Besides, I'm a Christian. I feel I should sympathize with rather than criticize feelings I do not agree with."

To me it takes a person with a right heart and an humble spirit not to respond aggressively to the types of incidents I just told about. I have frequently told white people on similar occasions I understood their feelings. I once had a long talk with a farmer in Chilton County one day. I told him that although not much had been said about the indignities that some whites had been subjected to, I knew that they too had been subjected to mistreatment just like blacks. I asked him if he could remember when state jobs were given only to the in-crowd of whites. This really got his attention, and he agreed that whites were subjected to injustices like blacks. He wanted to know my background. When I told him that I had been a teacher in the public school system of Montgomery, he said he knew that I wasn't an ordinary person. I did not consider a teacher's certificate and eight years of teaching experience would make me extraordinary as he seemed to think. Rather I felt what made me different was my relationship with God, the man upstairs.

I think back to the time when I first confessed Christ. It was a hot week following the second Sunday in August 1941. I had been on what was called the mourner's bench all week. I had sat on the mourner's bench the previous year, too, but at age twelve children were expected to confess Christ and join the church during annual revival. All of my life, I had been led to believe that religion was serious business and God was someone you did not play with. I was led to believe that when a person had been saved from his sins God would either speak to him plainly or would show him some kind of sign to let him know his soul was saved from eternal hell. God spoke to me through my conscience. I thought, *Have you been listening to the minister all week? He has said over and over again, "Only believe, Arthur Worthy." You're making something difficult out of something that is very simple. Who are you that God has to stop the sun from shining at midday to convince you that you have been saved? Only believe, it's just that simple.* When the minister concluded his sermon that afternoon and opened the doors of the church, I got up immediately and joined, confessing Christ. The minister asked the person joining, "Do you believe in Jesus? Has he forgiven you for your sins?" The joiner had to respond "yes" to both questions. In some churches the new member had to give a long testimony about being saved, but no verbal confession or statement was required in my church.

I stood up and was saved in Marengo County, Alabama, in August 1941, some four months before Pearl Harbor and the start of World War II. I have been telling most young people with whom I come in contact that life is a lot simpler than most of us make it. Throughout my life, I have found this to be true. I have had so very many experiences. Some of them sound like fiction or something out of a movie. It is not easy to believe that a child being physically punished by his teacher would defend his teacher's action to the supervisor or that a Southern white, during the days of extreme racial strife, would not be offended by a black law enforcement officer serving him with papers that force him to integrate the races or that three convicted bank robbers, after freeing themselves by grabbing a gun from one of the deputies guarding them would walk some 150 yards to get overcoats for their captors so they would not freeze to death. This is not a movie or television or fiction. These events are God's gift to Arthur Worthy.

I do not consider myself exceptional except for the fact that I know God and am guided by His direction in my life. I know the blessings that He has bestowed upon me as evidence of that connection, and I share the experiences that I have had over the past seventy-one years as a testimony to the power of God and the way he has made simple what might have been difficult. To those who profess Christianity or belief in Christ, I would like to say the church is not the only place to find the opportunity to serve Christ. Recently, I went with a group of deacons and ministers to serve communion to some older members who had been sick for a period of time and missed communion for a number of months. I said to one of the members who had been served communion in her home, "Sister X, I feel it is my Christian duty to come and cut the lawn when the lawn needs mowing. Call me, and I'll gladly come cut it." It is my sincere feeling that witnessing to Christ is not limited to the verbal. Sometimes action is needed. We must remember that God has no hands but our hands, no feet but our feet. It is my prayer that God will use me as the answer to someone's prayer. I believe that whatever difficulties that I may have to experience in my remaining years are not punishments or injustices, but God's will. I do not profess to understand God's will, but I accept it without question.

# VI

# FINAL DAYS

I T WAS MY DESIRE when these memoirs first got started that this chapter would not be written. You probably have noticed from the previous sections that I always had many things going on at the same time. You may have also noticed that if someone came to me for help, everything was stopped and I would go to the aid of the person requesting the aid. A little over a year ago, I got a real excuse, health failure. I was diagnosed as having a mini-stroke. There was no complete paralysis, but the use of my left leg and arm was slightly impaired. I received extensive medical examinations. I even went to medical clinics in other cities. Before the mini stroke, I had other health problems. I went to New York City to a clinic after some cancer cells were found while I was having a colon resection operation.

After the mini stroke, I have been to numerous doctors almost constantly. Some of these doctors determined that the mini stroke had caused the onset of dementia. I was told that dementia was not Alzheimer's as the back lobe of the brain was not affected. My frontal lobe had been affected. *Good*, I thought, *I do not have Alzheimer's.* When I asked what I did have, the doctors said it was Pick's, a disease about which very little is known. I got some very disturbing information about the disease off the Internet. Maybe I should have gotten Alzheimer's, at least then I would not be aware of everything that is happening. My short-term memory has been drastically affected. A new acquaintance can tell me his or her name and five minutes later I cannot repeat it.

I can only thank God for my having decided long ago to enjoy the things that I had always desired before bad health took over my life. Years ago, we saw the wonderful Niagara Falls of New York, the romantic beaches of southern France, Nice and Cannes, the beautiful Acapulco, Mexico. In 1999, just before the onset of dementia, we were planning an African safari as this was something we had been thinking about for a long time. The political unrest in South African countries made us somewhat fearful of vacationing there. When we started planning the vacation, we ran into all kinds of problems. We were told how many vaccinations we would have to have because of the number of diseases we would be exposed to while there. We were also told we would have to take a few medications while we were in South Africa and more when we returned home. We finally decided that we were a little too old to jeopardize our health by taking such a vacation. We decided to visit Portugal, Spain, Morocco and a North African country instead. When we returned home, we learned that some American vacationers had been attacked by political extremists while on an African safari. What was even more frightening, they had been traveling with Grand Circle, the same travel agency we used. We decided God had been present in our decision not to go to South Africa.

This Pick's disease is bad, but when I consider what God has allowed me to enjoy during the last seventy-one years, I am embarrassed to complain. I was admitted to South Rehab Center in the fall of 2000 for rehabilitation from the mini stroke and the Pick's. The week I spent there made me realize that I had more to be thankful for than I had to complain about. All around me were patients ten to twenty years younger than I who were in much worse condition. There were patients with brain injuries who couldn't hold a conversation. Nothing they said made sense. Just being in the presence of these individuals was psychologically depressing for me. I feel my dementia has affected me more physically than mentally.

I accompanied my wife Mildred to take my eighty-year-old cousin and her seventy-six-year-old brother to the Veterans Hospital at Tuskegee, Alabama. We went to see their ninety-seven-year-old brother who is confined to the hospital. This all happened the day after spending the week at South Rehab Center. This visit confirmed to me that, in spite of my being almost unable to get up off the floor after a fall and unable to remember a new person's name five minutes after I've heard it, I am still blessed beyond millions and I have more to be thankful to God for than I have to complain about.

The greatest blessing I now enjoy is my lovely wife Mildred. You talk about a marriage made in heaven, this is it. There are very few marriages where both partners will readily agree about almost everything. The travel that we have done extensively is rare. In many instances if the wife desires travel, the husband will hate it or if the husband wants to travel, the wife will hate it. There are very few couples who will both agree to buy two vacation homes when their main income is from working on jobs. We had a little income from rental property, but there were very few years that we did not have a loss instead of a profit.

I am beginning to understand doctors' reluctance to elaborate on Pick's disease. The patient could not bear to know the real truth. I continue to get weaker. If I fall to the floor, I need five minutes to get up. Hopefully, I will be able to finish these memoirs. I fear that if I do not finish them shortly, they will not be completed. No one seems to understand my restlessness. They don't understand when I tell them I need rest from resting. It makes no sense, yet that is the way it is with me. Movement gives me strength.

My constant falling made it a necessity that I am in a location where there will be someone other than my lovely wife to help. She is unable to lift me. I now live in an assisted living facility for people like me who need constant help. When I reached my room the first day, I found my computer and its printer already set up. If these memoirs are completed and published, it would be the first time in history that anyone has ever finished a book from a nursing home after the onset of dementia/Pick's. If you find it hard to accept the preceding sentence because you think it hyperbolic, let me just say this is my way of writing. As I have learned, in doing anything, there is a right way, a wrong way, and there is Arthur Worthy's way.

# EPILOGUE

## By MILDRED WORTHY

D URING ARTHUR'S declining years when he was
unable to drive or attend First Baptist Church, his
own church, pastored by E. Baxter Morris, Community Congregational United Church of Christ and its
pastor, Bennie Liggins, took him into their care. He attended
Sunday services and Bible study in his wheel chair.

His grandson Wilson Sippial Jr. and his son-in-law Wilson Sippial always assisted me with getting him in and out of
the car and into the church. Later when his health failed to the
extent that he had to be lifted completely the ushers and/or
deacons of the church always watched for us and assisted. I
was most grateful and appreciative for the total support of the
Community Congregational Church family. They showed
total patience and tolerance with Arthur even when his speech
was almost incomprehensible. They listened to him express
his opinions no matter how long it took or how many times he
interrupted. Pastor Bennie Liggins and the deacons served

him communion each first Sunday, including after he was confined in the nursing home. They have been most attentive and supportive to both of us. I will forever be grateful for their Christian support.

Also, Highland Avenue Baptist Church and their pastor Norman Simmons were very kind and supportive to us including sending spiritually uplifting notes each Wednesday after prayer meeting. For their support, I am grateful.

As of the printing of this book, Arthur is totally bedridden and being cared for by the competent staff at Hillwood Terrace Nursing Home where he is receiving excellent care.

My thanks and appreciation go out to all those individuals and/or groups who have given us comfort and support during these last two years. You will always be in our hearts and prayers.

# Index